Fires

BY TAMI DEEDRICK

Steadwell Books

Raintree Steck-Vaughn Publishers
A Harcourt Company

Austin · New York
www.steck-vaughn.com

Nature
on the
Rampage

Published by Raintree Steck-Vaughn Publishers,
an imprint of Steck-Vaughn Company.
Library of Congress Cataloging-in-Publication Data
Deedrick, Tami.
    Fires/by Tami Deedrick.
        p.c.m.
    Includes index.
    Summary: Explains how fires start and describes their good
and bad effects.
    ISBN 0-7398-1798-1
    1. Fires--Juvenile literature. [1. Fires.] I. Title.
TH9148 .D424 2000
363.37--dc21

                                                            99-058673

Printed in the United States of America
10 9 8 7 6 5 4 3 2 1 LB 02 01 00

Produced by Compass Books
Photo Acknowledgments
Archive Photos/Reuters/Mike Andreas, 9, 18
Digital Stock, 6
Photo Network/Debra Conkey, 4; Lonnie Duka, 16
    Robert W. Ginn, 13; Mary Messenger, 20;
    MacDonald Photography, 22; Dede Gilman, 24;
    Phyllis Picardi, 27; Esbin-Anderson, 29
Root Resources/Stan Osolinski, cover, title page; 10
    (inset), 14; John Kohont, 10

Content Consultant
John L. Cochran
Fire Management Specialist
U.S. Fire Administration

CONTENTS

How Fire Works

Fire always has been important. Fire is the flame, light, and heat given off when something is burning. People warm themselves by fire. They cook with fire.

However, fire can be harmful. It can burn buildings, animals, and people. Property loss from fire costs billions of dollars each year.

Smoke from fire is poisonous. People can die from breathing smoke. About 7,000 people in the United States die in fires every year.

 Smoke from fire is poisonous.

FIRE TRIANGLE

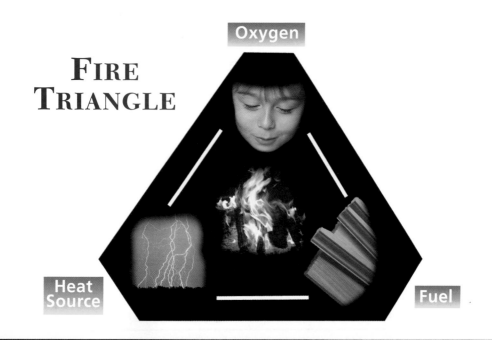

Oxygen

Heat
Source

Fuel

Fire Triangle

Fire needs three things to burn. Scientists call these three things the fire triangle. Fire needs oxygen. It needs fuel to burn. It needs a heat source to start. A fire will go out if one of these things is missing.

Oxygen keeps fire burning. This gas is in the air. Wind is one of the ways fire spreads.

Fuel is anything fire can burn. Fuel can be wood, grass, or leaves. Fire dies if it runs out of fuel.

Heat sources start fire. Sparks, volcano eruptions, and lightning are natural heat sources. Lightning is the most common natural heat source.

Some heat sources come from people. Ashes from cigarettes start some unwanted fires. Some children play with matches and cause fires. Firecrackers or bombs can start fires.

This diagram (top) shows the three things that make up the fire triangle. The fire (bottom) has all three things. This is why the fire keeps burning.

Planned and Unwanted Fires

Some fires are planned. People start planned fires on purpose. People set planned fires in forests to clear land for farming or travel. Campfires and fires in fireplaces and stoves are planned fires.

People control planned fires. They watch the fires. People put out the fires when they are done using them.

Unwanted fires happen by accident. People often are not careful with a heat source. Unwanted fires happen in offices and homes. They can happen on boats, airplanes, and in other places.

Wildfires happen in wilderness areas. Wildfires in forests are also called forest fires. The three kinds of forest fires are ground fires, surface fires, and crown fires.

Unwanted fires can happen in office buildings. A helicopter pours water on an unwanted fire in this bank in Jakarta, Indonesia.

Kinds of Forest Fires

Ground fire burns just underneath the ground. This fire is too low to receive much oxygen. Rotting plants and dead animals beneath the forest floor are fuel for ground fire. This slow-moving fire makes smoke and heat but little flame.

Ground fire can turn into surface fire. Surface fire burns above the ground. It burns grass, dead leaves, and fallen trees on the forest floor. Surface fire burns quickly and makes flames. It is the most common wildfire.

Surface fires sometimes find fire ladders. Fire ladders may be dry vines that wind around trees. They may be small trees that lead to the tops of tall trees. Surface fire burns its way up fire ladders. Treetops may catch fire. Surface fire then turns into crown fire.

Crown fire burns the tops of trees. Wind spreads crown fire from one tree to another. Winds can carry the fire over water. Some crown fires turn into firestorms.

Surface fire burns grass, leaves, and dead trees. Sometimes it burns its way up fire ladders (inset).

Firestorms

Firestorms are huge fires that make their own winds. Large streams of hot air rise during firestorms. Cool wind fills the space the hot air leaves. This movement of air makes strong winds. The winds in firestorms swirl. They suck everything nearby into the fire.

Firestorms can travel up to 100 miles (161 km) an hour. They can make walls of fire 100 feet (30 m) high. Smoke from firestorms is thick. Day seems like night.

Fire Damage

Fire can burn buildings and forests. It can melt plastics and metals. Fire also can burn skin. Most people die in fires from breathing smoke.

Fires sometimes cause more problems. Heavy rain after fires can cause landslides and floods. The ground cannot hold the water from the rain. Fires have burned all the trees and plants that soak up water.

Fire has destroyed this house in Atlanta, Georgia.

Fire Safety in a Building

People should leave buildings quickly if fires start. Fires burn quickly. People should not stay to save their belongings.

Feel the door before leaving a room. Do not open a hot door. Fire may be on the other side of the door. People should try to find another way out. Never ride elevators during a fire. The elevators may break down.

People should crawl out of burning buildings. Smoke rises to the top of a room. Staying low helps people breathe.

FIRE IN HISTORY

Fire is important to people. Early people had no electricity. They needed fire for heat and light. Early cities kept large fires burning all day and night. People watched the fires to make sure the fires did not die.

Some people used fire as a tool. American Indians burned forests so they could hunt more easily. They burned trees so grass would grow. Grass was the food of the bison, which many hunted.

A surface fire is burning its way up this tree. It will become a crown fire if it burns the top of the tree.

This fire is burning a prairie in the United States.

Fire Legends

Early people told stories to explain how fire first came to humans. A Greek story said the gods kept fire from humans. Prometheus was a cousin to the gods. He saw humans dying from cold.

Prometheus wanted people to have fire. He used a stick to catch fire from the sun. He brought the fiery stick to the cold caves where people lived. The people used the fire to warm themselves.

Creek people are American Indians. Their story said the weasels got fire when lightning struck a tree. But the weasels would not share fire. People were freezing.

Rabbit decided to help. He swam to the weasels' island. Rabbit set his own hair on fire. He kept part of his hair above water as he swam. He swam quickly to the people and gave them the fire.

Early Fires

Almost every country on Earth has had bad fires. A huge fire burned many buildings in Rome in 12 B.C. The fire made Emperor Augustus start one of the world's first fire departments. Another huge firestorm burned most of Rome in A.D. 64. The fire burned for eight days.

Fire destroyed 80 percent of London in 1666. The fire traveled along the banks of the Thames River. It burned everything in its path. The Duke of York created a firebreak by blowing up a row of houses. A firebreak is a band of ground where people remove anything that can burn. The fire stopped at the firebreak. About 200,000 people in London were homeless.

This map (above) shows the places of the fires written about in this book. The drawing below shows what the Great Chicago fire looked like.

The Great Chicago Fire of 1871

The Great Chicago Fire of 1871 started on October 8. Heat from the fire was so strong that it burned the hair of people standing in nearby Lake Michigan. They were in the lake to escape from the fire. The fire even burned the pipes of Chicago's water system. Firefighters had no water to fight the fire. It stopped only when there was nothing left to burn.

More than 300 people died in the Great Chicago fire. It cost more than $200 million to rebuild the city.

Peshtigo Fire of 1871

The deadliest firestorm in the United States also happened October 8, 1871, in Peshtigo, Wisconsin. The firestorm's winds ripped roofs from houses. Some people jumped into the Peshtigo River to escape the fire. But many people died by breathing in smoke. Many people burned to death.

The Peshtigo fire killed about 1,200 people. It burned down more than 2,400 acres (971 ha) of Wisconsin forests. It burned down entire towns. Only part of one wall remained in Peshtigo after the firestorm. The rest of the town was ashes.

FIRE TODAY

People learned from the 1871 fires. They invented better fire alarms. They built new water systems to help firefighters. They made new tools for firefighters to put out fires.

Today, people understand more about fires. They have better ways to prevent fires and fight fires. But fires still happen all around the world.

Fireworks began a major fire in Mexico City, Mexico, in December 1988. Many people were shopping for fireworks and Christmas presents. Some fireworks caught on fire. The whole market exploded with fireworks. More than 50 people died.

This firefighter is using a powerful hose to spray water on a fire in Sacramento, California.

Fire burned about half of Yellowstone National Park in 1988.

Wildfire Safety

People should build campfires away from trees and bushes. They must put out fires before leaving. Small fires left alone may turn into large wildfires.

People should look for water if they cannot escape from the fire. They should stay in water and cover their heads with wet clothes.

A bed of rocks is another place to hide from a fire. Fire cannot burn rocks. People should lie flat on the rocks. They should cover their heads with wet clothes or dirt. They should try not to breathe smoke.

Yellowstone National Park

Yellowstone National Park covers land in Idaho, Montana, and Wyoming. In 1972, park rangers decided to let wildfires burn. They put out fires only if they burned too close to people or buildings. From 1972 to 1987, they let more than 200 fires burn.

In June 1988, another fire started. Park rangers let the fire burn. They thought the fire would burn out. It did not. By August, more than 200,000 acres (80,940 ha) of the park had burned.

Officials did not want the whole park to burn. They began fighting the fire. The first snow in September finally slowed the fire. More than 1 million acres (404,700 ha) had burned. Today, new trees and plants grow in those areas.

FIRES AND SCIENCE

Scientists study fire. They learn about fuels. They study how winds spread fire. What they learn teaches people how to fight fires.

Ways to Fight Fires

Firefighters may pour water on fires to cool the fire's heat. Firefighters use special chemicals and foams to stop oxygen from feeding fires. The chemicals also cool fire.

Airplane and helicopter pilots may drop water and chemicals from the sky over large fires. The chemicals sometimes are colored red so pilots can see where chemicals have dropped.

 This helicopter pilot is trying to stop fire from burning nearby houses. The fire is in California.

Fire-Fighting Tools

Firefighters try to take away one of the three things fire needs. Firefighters may take away fuel. They sometimes make a firebreak. Firefighters may start a backfire to burn a wildfire's fuel. The backfire moves toward the approaching wildfire. As it moves, it burns all the fuel. Both fires go out when they meet.

Today, firefighters have many tools. Alarm systems tell firefighters where fires are. Sprinkler systems spray water on fires before firefighters arrive. Smoke alarms tell people if smoke is in their houses. Smoke can mean that fire is there too.

Some tools help people spot fires. Forest rangers have lookout towers to spot fires. Helicopters help find fires. Infrared cameras show areas of heat. Rangers use these cameras to find fires hidden by smoke or bad weather.

Satellites in space help find fires. Satellites can take pictures and send information back to Earth. Satellites can show exactly where and how big a fire is.

These firefighters are trying to stop a house fire in Georgia.

Stop, Drop, and Roll

People must stop if their clothes catch fire. They should drop to the ground and roll on the floor. Rolling keeps oxygen from feeding the fire. A fire only will only get bigger if people move or run. Running gives a fire a lot of oxygen.

Fire Ecology

Fire ecologists try to learn how fire changes people, animals, and plants. These scientists understand that fire helps keep nature healthy.

Fire is important to the growth of a forest. A fire burns the waste on the forest floor. It turns dead plants into nutrients for the soil. Nutrients are minerals that help plants grow healthy and strong.

Some kinds of plants and trees are fire species. Fire species need fire to grow. Fireweed is a colorful plant that grows right after a fire burns. Ponderosa and lodgepole pines need fire to reproduce. The seeds of these pines have flammable coverings. Flammable means able to catch fire easily. Fire melts the coverings. Seeds then fall to the ground and grow new trees.

Fires will continue to cause damage. Scientists hope to learn more about controlling fire. They want to learn how to fight unwanted fires better. This will save people and property.

Fireweed is growing in parts of Yosemite National Park that have been burned by fire.

GLOSSARY

crown fire (CROWN FIRE)—fire that burns the tops of trees

firebreak (FIRE-brake)—a band of ground where the fuel for a fire has been removed

firestorm (FIRE-storm)—a huge fire that makes its own winds

ground fire (GROWND FIRE)—fire that burns just below the forest floor

heat source (HEET SORSS)—heat that starts a fire

nutrient (NOO-tree-uhnt)—a mineral that helps plants grow

satellite (sa-TUH-lite)—equipment sent into space to circle Earth; some satellites take pictures or record information about Earth.

surface fire (SUR-fass FIRE)—fire that burns dead plants and trees on the forest floor

U.S. Fire Administration
16825 South Seton Avenue
Emmitsburg, MD 21727

USDA Forest Service
P.O. Box 96090
Washington, DC 20090-6090

FEMA for Kids: Wildfire
http://www.fema.gov/kids/wldfire.htm

Fire Admistration's Kids Page
http://www.usfa.fema.gov/kids/

The Great Chicago Fire
http://www.chicagohs.org/fire/intro

Newton's Apple: Firefighting
http://ericir.syr.edu/Projects/Newton/11/fire.html

INDEX

American Indians, 15, 17

backfire, 26
bison, 15

Chicago, Illinois, 19
cigarettes, 7
crown fire, 8, 11

fire ladder, 11
fire species, 28
fire triangle, 7
firebreak, 17, 26
firecracker, 7
firestorm, 11, 12, 17, 19
fireweed, 28
fireworks, 21
flood, 12
forest fire, 8

Greek, 16
ground fire, 8, 11

infrared cameras, 26

landslide, 12
lightning, 7
London, England, 17
lookout towers, 26

matches, 7
Mexico City, Mexico, 21

oxygen, 7, 11, 25, 27

Peshtigo, Wisconsin, 19
Prometheus, 16

Rome, 17

satellites, 26
surface fire, 8, 11

Yellowstone National Park, 23